PART ONE

LAND OF LIBERTY?

The men, women and children in this photograph are immigrants to the United States of America – the 'New World' – around 1900. They have just arrived by ship in New York to start new lives as American citizens. Over the years, millions like them have already settled in the New World, and millions more will follow them.

What has brought these people to America? What is the attraction of a country they have never seen before, and where they have no friends, no home and no work?

In many cases these people have left their own countries because they believe that America is a land of opportunity. The United States was founded by people who believed in freedom and equality. In their famous Declaration of Independence in 1776 they wrote:

'We hold these truths to be evident, that all men are created equal, that they are endowed by their creator with certain inalienable rights [*rights that cannot be taken away*]. Among these are Life, Liberty and the Pursuit of Happiness.'

In the 'Pursuit of Happiness', many immigrants had already found success. America was a land where, with a bit of luck and a lot of hard work, anyone could become rich. Every day, a flood of new immigrants arrived in America's sea ports, filled with this American dream.

This book invites you to find out whether America in the 1920s really did provide its people with the liberty and happiness they dreamed about. We will begin with the dream of liberty.

1

HOW AMERICA IS GOVERNED: THE CONSTITUTION

'My country! 'tis of thee,
Sweet Land of Liberty,
Of thee I sing.
Land where my fathers died!
Land of the Pilgrims' pride!
From every mountain side
Let freedom ring!'

These lines are from 'America', a patriotic American song. It has the same tune as the British national anthem. One reason why Americans call their country a 'land of liberty' is their democratic system of government. Before going any further we need to understand how America is governed.

A union of states

The USA was born on 4 July 1774 when thirteen British colonies in North America declared that they wanted to be independent. After fighting a War of Independence against Britain, the Americans joined the thirteen colonies together into a new nation, the United States of America. The original thirteen states are remembered by the thirteen stripes on the American flag. Since then, other states have been formed and have joined the union. Now there are fifty states, represented by fifty stars on the flag.

The Constitution

Soon after winning independence the Americans drew up a **Constitution**. The Constitution is a set of rules describing how America must be governed. Part of it, called the **Bill of Rights**, also describes the rights of the people.

The constitution describes a **federal** system of government. This means that the job of running the country is divided between two kinds of government – the central, or federal, government in Washington, and the local governments of each of the fifty states.

As you can see from the diagram opposite, there are three branches of the federal government. The **legislative** branch makes the country's laws, the

The United States of America

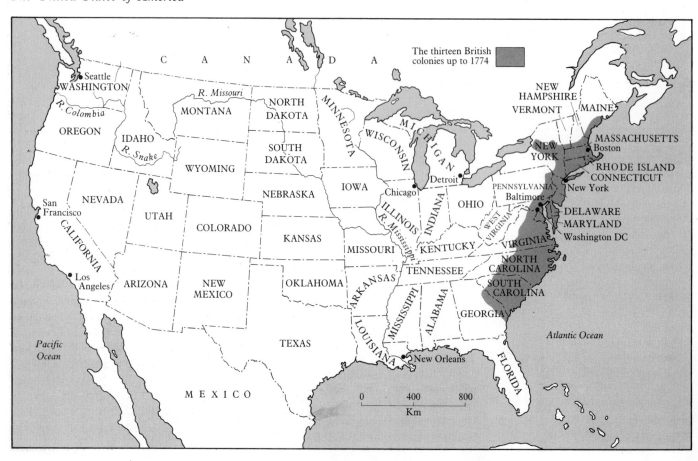

executive branch carries out these laws, and the **judiciary** makes sure the laws are obeyed. Nobody is allowed to belong to more than one of these branches, so nobody can get too much power.

The fifty state governments are also divided into three branches. Each state has a Governor at the head of the executive branch, a legislature for making state laws, and a system of state courts. In each state the laws are different, so gambling is against the law in some states but quite legal in others. The police of one state cannot chase a criminal into another state. Only federal police, such as the FBI (Federal Bureau of Investigation), can cross state borders.

Democracy

The American system of government is a **democracy**. This means that all adults in America have certain equal rights. The first is the right to vote. Americans vote in elections for the President and for Congress. They also vote in local elections for their state Governors and Legislatures, and for public officials such as the judges of law courts.

In addition to the right to vote, Americans have many rights which safeguard their freedom. These are listed in the Bill of Rights. They have the rights of free speech and a free press, as well as the right of free assembly – the right to meet and form groups such as trade unions. The Bill of Rights even gives them the right to carry weapons to protect themselves.

In elections, voters have two main political parties to choose between. The **Democratic Party** tends to be liberal – it favours helping the poor and the old, for example. The **Republican Party** is more conservative – it often supports businessmen and wealthy people.

The system of federal government

The legislative branch	The executive branch	The judicial branch
Congress makes laws. It is the American parliament and has two houses.	*President* Elected every four years. The President is • Commander-in-Chief of the army and navy; • head of government (like the British Prime Minister); • head of state (like the British monarch).	*Supreme Court* Nine judges appointed by the President. Their job is to make sure that Congress and the President run the country according to the Constitution.
House of Representatives 435 members, or 'Congressmen'. Each Congressman represents about 450,000 voters. They are elected for two years. *Senate* 100 members, or 'Senators'. There are two Senators from each state. They are elected for six years.	*Cabinet* A group of advisers to the President, called Secretaries. They are like Ministers in the British government.	

Work section

A. Test your understanding of this chapter by choosing five words from column B that match the descriptions in column A.

A1 A system of government in which the fifty state governments share power with the central government in Washington	B1 Congress
A2 The set of rules describing how America is governed and what rights people have	B2 Cabinet
	B3 Federal
A3 Nine judges who make sure that the country is run according to the constitution	B4 Supreme Court
	B5 Constitution
A4 A group of Presidential advisers called Secretaries	B6 Democracy
A5 The parliament of America	B7 Senate
	B8 Republican

B. Study the table above showing the system of federal government. List the parts of the system which are similar to the British system of government, then list the parts which are unlike the British system.

2

HOW AMERICA IS GOVERNED: THE PRESIDENTS OF THE 1920s

As you have found out, the President of America has a great deal of power. He is Commander-in-Chief of the armed forces, head of state and head of the government. He is the most powerful elected leader in the world. What kind of men held this important office during the 1920s?

Woodrow Wilson, 1913–21

In 1920 the American President was a Democrat, Woodrow Wilson. Under his leadership, America had entered the Great War in 1917 on the side of the Allies. In 1919, when the war was over, Wilson went to Paris to help draw up peace treaties.

Wilson's main aim at the Paris Peace Conference was to set up a world peace-keeping organisation. He succeeded, and a **League of Nations** was created in 1920.

But the Republican Party in Congress did not want America to join the League of Nations. There was a strong feeling throughout the country that America should have nothing more to do with the affairs of Europe.

Wilson tried to get support for joining the League by going on a tour of America, making speeches. But half way through his tour Wilson collapsed with a stroke. Now he was an invalid, paralysed down one side of his body. While he lay ill in the White House, the Senate voted against joining the League of Nations. It was the start of a period of **isolation** in American history, when America kept out of the affairs of other countries as far as possible.

In November 1920 there was an election for the Presidency. Wilson was too ill to stand for re-election. Anyway, the voters had turned against his ideas of peace and international brotherhood. With a record number of votes they elected a Republican, Warren G. Harding, to be their next President.

Warren G. Harding, 1921–3

When Harding won the election, one Republican Senator said 'Harding is no world-beater. But he's the best of the second-raters'.

Harding knew he was not a brilliant politician, so he gave the best jobs in the Cabinet to first-rate politicians who knew what they were doing. However, he also gave important jobs to his friends. They were known as the **Ohio Gang**, after the state

of Ohio that Harding came from. The Ohio Gang was soon meeting in the White House to do the things that Harding liked best – drinking whisky and playing poker for high stakes.

Several members of the Ohio Gang were very dishonest. Charles Forbes, Harding's closest friend, was the director of a government department called the Veterans' Bureau. His job was to take care of disabled American soldiers. During his two years as director, over $200 million of the Bureau's money disappeared, much of it into Forbes's pockets.

Another member of the Ohio Gang, Albert Fall, sold an oil company the right to drill for oil at **Teapot Dome** in the state of Wyoming. The oil was not his to sell, for Teapot Dome was government-owned land. Albert Fall made $100,000 out of the deal.

The public knew almost nothing of these scandals while Harding was President. Harry Daugherty, the Attorney-General at the head of the American legal system, was one of the Ohio Gang, and he managed to cover up the scandals for several years.

Warren Harding was a popular President. He promised to take America 'back to normalcy'. This meant getting back to the kind of life that the Great War had interrupted. Americans could now concentrate on building up the country and making themselves prosperous instead of being involved in foreign affairs.

Harding died suddenly of a stroke in 1923 and was succeeded by his deputy, Vice-President Calvin Coolidge.

Calvin Coolidge, 1923–9

Calvin Coolidge was mean and dull, and he said very little. For this reason he was known as 'Silent Cal'.

One of the things that 'Silent Cal' did say was 'the business of America is business'. He meant that Americans should concentrate on making themselves prosperous – by setting up companies, by investing money, and by working hard.

Under Coolidge, many Americans became rich. This was not due to him, however. As a Republican, he believed that the government should not interfere in people's lives. He therefore did very little as President, working an average of only four hours a day. The people who got rich did so by their own efforts.

Coolidge was an honest man and one of the few

4

things he did as President was to sack Harding's friends from their government posts. Several of them were put on trial and sent to prison.

By election year, 1928, America was the richest country in the world. Coolidge, however, did not want to stand for re-election. A millionaire businessman, Herbert Hoover, stood in his place and won easily.

Herbert Hoover, 1929–33

Herbert Hoover was a Republican. Like Coolidge he thought that the government should not interfere in people's lives. He believed in what he called '**rugged individualism**' – people working hard for themselves, and not relying on the government for help. Hoover had started life as a mining engineer and had retired as a multi-millionaire by the age of forty. If he could climb from rags to riches by his own efforts, so could anyone else, he thought.

Unfortunately an economic depression hit America while Hoover was President. By 1932 over twelve million Americans were out of work and living in dreadful poverty. The Republican idea of 'rugged individualism' had no value when there was no work for people to do.

Work section

A. For each of the Presidents named in column A, select three statements from column B that describe them accurately.

A1 Woodrow Wilson
A2 Warren Harding
A3 Calvin Coolidge
A4 Herbert Hoover

B1 A multi-millionaire by the age of forty
B2 A Republican
B3 Promised a return to 'normalcy' after the Great War
B4 Did little and said little
B5 Led America to war in 1917
B6 A Republican
B7 A poker player with dishonest friends
B8 America became the richest country in the world while he was President
B9 A Democrat
B10 Believed in 'rugged individualism'
B11 Helped create the League of Nations
B12 A Republican

B. Study this American cartoon of 1926. Then, using the information you have read in this chapter, answer the following questions.
1. Who is the man trying to hold the door shut? What was his position in the American government?
2. To which years do you think 'THE PAST', written on the door, refers? What was there in 'the past' that this man did not want to escape?
3. Explain in your own words what you think the cartoonist was getting at.

C. Before going any further, make notes on what you have read so far in this book. There is a revision guide on page 14 to help you.

3

'PURE AMERICANISM': RACIAL PROBLEMS IN THE 1920s

Immigration

Most Americans are immigrants to their country. The 'Pilgrim Fathers' who sailed to America on the *Mayflower* in 1620 were some of the earliest immigrants. Since then, many millions of people from Europe, Asia and Africa have migrated to America.

By 1920 American society was made up of more colours and more religions and spoke more languages than any other country in the world. Many white English-speaking Americans disliked this. Over the years the white Americans had become the most powerful group in American society, owning more land, earning more money, and having more power than anyone else. They saw Jews, blacks, Catholics and foreigners of all kinds as a threat to their supremacy. Most of all they disliked blacks and immigrants from central Europe and from Russia.

To cut down the number of immigrants to America, Congress passed a series of **Immigration Laws**. The 1917 Immigration Law said that immigrants must pass a literacy test, showing that they could read and write, before they could enter the country. In 1921 the Immigration Quota Act declared that no more than 357,000 immigrants could enter America each year. Two more Immigration Acts in 1924 and 1929 cut this figure to 150,000.

The Ku Klux Klan

The Immigration Acts cut down the rate of immigration, but they did not stop many white Americans from hating the immigrants who already lived there. Between 1920 and 1925 around five million white Americans joined a secret society called the **Ku Klux Klan**. Named after the Greek word for circle, *Kuklos*, the Ku Klux Klan stirred up racial and religious hatred wherever it could. Its aims can be seen in this extract from its book of rules, the *Kloran*.

A. '1. Is the motive prompting you to be a Klansman serious and unselfish?
2. Are you a native born, white, gentile [*non-Jewish*] American?
3. Are you absolutely opposed to and free of any allegiance of any nature to any cause, government, people, sect or ruler that is foreign to the United States of America?
4. Do you believe in the tenets [*beliefs*] of the Christian religion? . . .
8. Do you believe in and will you faithfully strive for the eternal maintenance of white supremacy?'

The Ku Klux Klan was strongest in the southern states where there was a large black population. The leader of the Klan, a dentist from Texas named Hiram Wesley Evans, called the South 'the Invisible Empire'. He himself was the 'Imperial Wizard' of the Empire. Local units of the Empire were called 'Dens'. Each Den was run by an 'Exalted Cyclops' and members had titles such as 'Kludds', 'Kligrapps', and 'Klabees'. The Klansmen, disguised in white robes and hoods, spoke to each other in codes known as 'Klonversations':

B. *The Ku Klux Klan swearing in a new member in November 1922. Note the American flag and the burning cross being held above his head*

C. *Two black Americans lynched by a mob in the Southern States, late 1920s*

D. '*Ayak*: Are you a Klansman?
Akia: A Klansman I am.
Capowe: Countersign and password or written evidence . . .
No. 1 Atga: Number one Klan of Atlanta, Georgia.
Kigy: Klansman, I greet you.'

The secret codes of the Ku Klux Klan may be amusing, but their activities were far from funny. Many 'dens' used torture and violence against people they said were 'unamerican'. The following acts of violence were carried out by the Ku Klux Klan in Alabama:

E. 'A lad whipped with branches until his back was ribboned flesh; a negress beaten and left helpless to contract pneumonia from exposure and die; a white girl, divorcee, beaten into unconsciousness in her own home; a naturalised foreigner flogged until his back was a pulp because he married an American woman; a negro lashed until he sold his land to a white woman for a fraction of its value.'

Back to Africa?

Black Americans tried to improve their conditions in the 1920s by setting up reform associations. The **NAACP**, the National Association for the Advancement of Colored People, urged the government to improve their conditions by introducing new laws. In particular, they wanted a law against lynching, for many blacks were hung from trees by the Ku Klux Klan during the 1920s. They also wanted a law giving all black people the right to vote; many were stopped from voting by unfair local laws such as the 'grandfather clause' which said that anyone whose grandfather had been a slave did not have voting rights. The government, however did not introduce any of the laws that the NAACP wanted.

Some black people believed that the NAACP would never be able to improve their conditions. They listened instead to the words of Marcus Garvey who started a '**Back to Africa**' movement. His plan was for black people to return to Africa where they had originally lived before being taken to America as slaves. In Africa they would create a black empire. The movement failed after Garvey was imprisoned for fraud.

Work section

A. Test your understanding of this chapter by explaining the following terms: immigration; Ku Klux Klan; 'Back to Africa'.

B. Study sources A, B, C and D. Judging by this evidence, describe the kind of person who might have been tempted to join the Ku Klux Klan in the 1920s.

C. Study source E.
1. According to this evidence, why did the Ku Klux Klan beat the 'naturalised foreigner' and the 'negro'?
2. Why do you think the Ku Klux Klan beat 'the lad', 'the negress' and the 'white girl, divorcee'?
3. Why do you think the Ku Klux Klan used such violent methods?
4. Suggest as many reasons as you can to explain why the Ku Klux Klan was able to get away with such violent actions without being punished.

THE BIG RED SCARE: POLITICAL INTOLERANCE IN THE 1920s

In 1920 some 150,000 Americans were communists or anarchists – people who believed in overthrowing the government in a violent revolution. They were divided into thirty-two different groups, the smallest of which had two members. They formed 0.1 per cent of the population and, as an American journalist later wrote, 'the whole lot were about as dangerous as a flea on an elephant'.

But many Americans were scared of the communists and anarchists, however harmless they were. Partly this was because communists had overthrown the Russian government in 1917 and were now the rulers of Russia. Americans feared that communism would spread from Russia. They also had a reason to fear the anarchists: only twenty years earlier, in 1901, an anarchist shot President William McKinley dead.

In 1919 fear of the 'Reds', as communists were known, increased when trade unions organised a series of strikes. Hundreds of thousands of steel workers and coal miners went on strike. So too did the entire police force of Boston, demanding wage rises. Public opinion blamed the strikes on communist agents and trouble-makers.

The Palmer Raids of 1920

The politician A. Mitchell Palmer hated the 'Reds'. He was the United States Attorney-General, the member of the Cabinet in charge of America's law and police. Late at night in July 1919, while he was on his way to bed, an exploding bomb ripped out the front of Palmer's house. The limbs of a man blown to pieces were found outside, along with a copy of *Plain Words*, a communist newspaper.

The explosion was the latest in a series of bomb attacks on politicians. Palmer blamed the 'Reds' and decided to get rid of them. On New Year's Day 1920 Palmer began a series of police raids on the homes of suspected communists and anarchists. Over 6000 people were arrested and put in prison.

Palmer had to release most of the prisoners within a few weeks. The police could find no evidence that they had committed any crime. During the raids, all the police found were three pistols. They found no explosives.

The American people were so scared of a communist revolution that few protested against the Palmer raids – even though America's leading law officer had

Nicola Sacco and Bartolomeo Vanzetti, after hearing that their appeal for a new trial had been turned down

A protest demonstration in April 1927 against the decision to execute Sacco and Vanzetti

wrongly arrested 6000 innocent people. Many people did, however, protest against another case of wrongful arrest in 1920.

The Sacco and Vanzetti Case

On 5 May 1920 Nicola Sacco and Bartolomeo Vanzetti were arrested and charged with a wages robbery in which two guards were shot dead. Sacco and Vanzetti were immigrants from Italy, living in Massachusetts. Neither spoke English well. Both were anarchists. And when they were arrested, both were carrying loaded guns.

Sacco and Vanzetti were put on trial in front of Judge Webster Thayer. A leading American lawyer said this about him:

> 'I have known Judge Thayer all my life . . . I say that he is a narrow-minded man; he is a half educated man; he is an unintelligent man; he is full of prejudice; he is carried away by fear of Reds, which [has] captured about ninety per cent of the American people.'

Four kinds of evidence were used against Sacco and Vanzetti in their trial. First, both men were carrying loaded guns when they were arrested. Second, the bullets in Sacco's gun were the same size as those which killed the guards. Third, Sacco had leaflets in his pocket advertising an anarchist meeting when he was arrested. And fourth, sixty-one eye witnesses of the wages robbery identified Sacco and Vanzetti as the killers.

The defence evidence consisted of statements that the two men were elsewhere at the time of the robbery. One hundred and seven witnesses swore to seeing them elsewhere. The jury was not convinced and found both men guilty of murder.

Sacco and Vanzetti stayed in prison for the next seven years while their lawyer appealed against the verdict. Outside prison, many people organised demonstrations and petitions in Sacco and Vanzetti's support. They believed that Sacco and Vanzetti had been found guilty because they were foreign and because they were anarchists.

But it was no use. Judge Thayer turned down every appeal and sentenced both men to death. They were executed by electric chair on 24 August 1927.

Work section

A. Give three reasons why many Americans were scared of 'Reds' in 1920.

B. 'Although people are still divided about the guilt or innocence of Sacco and Vanzetti, there is now little doubt that the two men were denied the fair trial guaranteed by the Bill of Rights' (Ernest R. May, an American historian).
Judging by what you have read in this chapter, do you agree that Sacco and Vanzetti were not given a fair trial? Explain your answer.

C. Study the photograph above then answer these questions:
1. To which political party do you think the men holding placards belonged? Explain your answer.
2. Judging by what you have read in this chapter, why do you think so many people protested against the death sentences on Sacco and Vanzetti?

9

5

PROHIBITION, GANGSTERS AND VIOLENCE

Study this poster. It was issued in 1910 by the **Anti-Saloon League**, a religious organisation that wanted to ban alcoholic drink everywhere in America.

SLAVES OF THE SALOON

The saloon business cannot exist without slaves. You may smile at that statement, but it is absolutely true. Is not the man who is addicted to the drink habit a slave? There are 1,000,000 such slaves in the United States. They are slaves of the saloon. They go out and work a week or a month, draw their pay, go into the saloon, and hand the saloon keeper their money for something which ruins their own lives. Is not this slavery? Has there ever been in the history of the world a worse system of slavery? It is quite natural, of course, that the slaveholder should not care to liberate these slaves.— *Richmond P. Hobson.*

A woman entered a barroom, and advanced quietly to her husband, who sat drinking with three other men. "Thinkin' ye'd be too busy to come home to supper, Jack, I've fetched it to you here."
And she departed. The man laughed awkwardly. He invited his friends to share the meal with him. Then he removed the cover from the dish. The dish was empty. It contained a slip of paper that said: "I hope you will enjoy your supper. It is the same your wife and children have at home."— *Chicago Chronicle.*

The liquor traffic, like the slave trade or piracy, cannot be mended, and therefore must be actually ended.— *Joseph Cook.*

The Anti-Saloon League had a lot of support. By the time America went to war in 1917, eighteen states had already banned alcohol.

The war against Germany helped the Anti-Saloon League to win its fight to make all states 'dry'. Many American brewers were German immigrants, so the League claimed that people who drank beer were traitors to their country. Congress agreed with this anti-German view and in 1918 amended, or changed, the Constitution to prohibit Americans from making, selling or moving alcoholic drinks.

Prohibition

The Eighteenth Amendment to the Constitution stated that '. . . the manufacture, sale or transportation of intoxicating liquors within . . . the United States . . . for beverage purposes is hereby prohibited'. A separate law called the **Volstead Act** defined 'intoxicating liquor' as any liquid containing more than half a per cent of alcohol.

Prohibition, as this ban on alcohol was known, came into force in January 1920. Almost immediately people began to break the new law. Secret saloon bars called **speakeasies** opened up in cellars and back rooms. They had names like the 'Dizzy Club' and the 'Sligo Slasher's', and drinkers had to give passwords or knock at the door in code to be let in.

Speakeasies sold 'bootleg' alcohol. Smugglers, called '**bootleggers**', smuggled it into America from abroad. They also sold 'moonshine', a spirit made secretly in home-made stills. Drinkers could also buy 'near-beer', an alcohol-free beer allowed by the Volstead Act.

The failure of prohibition

Prohibition never worked. In a single year, 1925, Americans drank 200 million gallons of spirits, 685

Inside a speakeasy

million gallons of malt liquor and 118 million gallons of wine. By 1933 there were 200,000 speakeasies in America. In New York alone there were 32,000 speakeasies, whereas before prohibition there had been only 15,000 saloons.

There were two main reasons why prohibition failed. First, there were not enough officials to enforce it. America has a border 30,000 km long and a population of over 100 million. But there were only 4500 Prohibition agents to stop smugglers and to raid speakeasies.

Prohibition also failed because gangs of criminals moved into the bootleg business. They made so much money that they could bribe the authorities – police, judges and state officials – to cooperate with them.

Al Capone and gangster violence

The most powerful of the gangs was based in Chicago and was led by **Al Capone**. By 1927 he was earning some $60 million a year from bootlegging. His gang was like a private army; he had 700 men under his command, many of them armed with sawn-off shot-guns and Thompson sub-machine guns – 'Chicago typewriters' as they called them. One by one, Capone's rivals were slaughtered. 227 rival gangsters were 'rubbed out' in four years. On a single day, 14 February 1929, Capone's men machine-gunned seven members of the Bugs Moran gang in the St Valentine Day's Massacre.

Gangs were not only involved in bootlegging. They also made money out of **rackets**. Businessmen and shopkeepers had to pay 'protection money' to gangsters to prevent their premises from being smashed up by the gang's 'education committee'. Capone made a further $10 million a year from racketeering.

Capone was able to get away with crime because he had Chicago's police and politicians in his pay.

Over half the police force took bribes from him. Even though Capone was 'Public Enemy Number One', judges and police chiefs socialised with him at cock-tail parties and called him Al.

It was the federal government that finally dealt with Capone. In 1931 he was found guilty of tax evasion and sentenced to eleven years in prison.

'Public enemy number one' makes the front cover of Time, *a leading American weekly magazine, 1930*

Work section

A. Test your understanding of this chapter by explaining the following terms: the Eighteenth Amendment; the Volstead Act; speakeasies; bootleggers; moonshine; gangs; rackets.

B. Study the Anti-Saloon League poster opposite. For what reasons, according to this evidence, did the League want to ban alcohol?

C. 'I call myself a businessman. I make my money by supplying a popular demand. If I break the law, my customers are as guilty as I am' (Al Capone).
   1. What was the 'popular demand' that Al Capone supplied? How much money did he make out of supplying it?
   2. For what reasons could Al Capone be called a businessman? What other terms could be used accurately to describe him?
   3. What do you think Capone meant by 'my customers are as guilty as I am'? Do you think this was a fair statement? Explain your answer.

D. Look at the picture above.
   1. Why is it surprising to see a photograph of Al Capone on the front cover of a leading magazine?
   2. What does it tell you about the way in which Capone was regarded by Americans in the 1920s?

6

THE MONKEY TRIAL: RELIGIOUS PROBLEMS IN THE 1920s

In the 1920s most communities in the American countryside were very religious. Country people prided themselves on being god-fearing, church-going Christians. In the cities, however, church attendance was falling. To try and stop this, a number of **revivalist** groups were formed, groups which aimed to revive interest in the Christian faith.

The revivalists

The best known revivalist of the 1920s was Aimee Semple McPherson. Sister Aimee, as she called herself, was head of the 'Four Square Gospel Alliance'. Her church, the Angelus Temple in Los Angeles, held 5000 people for services. Sister Aimee, often dressed as an angel, led the congregation in hymn singing, beating time with a tambourine. Every evening she baptised 150 people in a giant tank of water in the temple. She healed incurably ill people and filled the 'Miracle Room' of the Temple with discarded crutches and wheelchairs. Within five years she had built up a large fortune and was famous throughout the world.

Sister Aimee preaching in the Angelus Temple

Billy Sunday in a typical pose, 1928

Another famous revivalist, Billy Sunday, specialised in preaching hell-fire sermons from the pulpit. Like Sister Aimee, he became a millionaire as a result of collections taken among his audiences.

The fundamentalists

Over half the Christians in America belonged to Protestant churches such as the Baptist and Meth-odist churches. But Protestants in the 1920s split into two groups which disagreed with each other about the **theory of evolution**, an explanation of the way in which life on earth has developed.

Charles Darwin, in his book *The Origin of Species*, argued that life on earth began many millions of years ago and that it developed slowly into its present form. Human beings, he said, developed gradually from the same origins as other animals. So human beings have the same ancestors as, say, apes. Many people thought Darwin meant that humans evolved from monkeys.

Darwin's theory of evolution caused bitter arguments as soon as it appeared in 1859. The arguments were still raging in rural America at the start of the twentieth century. Many American Protestants thought that the theory was an attack on the Holy Bible. According to the Bible, God created the universe and everything in it in six days. A careful reading of the Bible suggests that this happened in the year 4004 BC.

In 1919 Protestants who believed this biblical explanation of the origins of the world set up 'The World's Christian Fundamentals Association'. The aim of these **fundamentalists** was to make Darwin's theory of evolution illegal.

In 1924 the fundamentalists set up an **Anti-Evolution League**. 'Flying Fundamentalists' toured America making speeches against Darwin. Gradually they began to succeed in their aim. Six states passed laws making it illegal for teachers to teach the theory of evolution.

One of the states that passed an anti-evolution law was Tennessee. The Tennessee law stated that:

> 'It shall be unlawful for any teacher . . . to teach any theory that denies the story of the divine creation of man as taught in the bible, and to teach instead that man has descended from a lower order of animals.'

Johnny Scopes and the 'Monkey Trial'

As soon as the law was passed, two men in Dayton, a small town in Tennessee, decided to put the law to the test. One of the men was a twenty-four-year-old biology teacher called Johnny Scopes. He agreed to teach the theory of evolution to one of his classes and to let his friend sue him for breaking the law.

Johnny Scopes taught a class the theory of evolution and was promptly arrested. A leading fundamentalist, William Jennings Bryan, was called

A street in Dayton, Tennessee, during the 'Monkey Trial' of Johnny Scopes in July 1925

in to be the prosecutor at Scopes's trial. A lawyer named Clarence Darrow was hired to defend Scopes. Bryan and Darrow were the most famous lawyers in America, and pressmen from all over the world gathered in Dayton to report the trial.

In the 'Monkey Trial', as people called it, Darrow questioned Bryan about his fundamentalist beliefs. He asked him how he thought the world was created. Bryan said that God had created the world in 4004 BC. Darrow asked:

'Do you say you do not believe that there are any civilisations on this earth that reach back beyond five thousand years?'

Bryan replied:

'I am not satisfied by any evidence I have seen.'

Bryan went on to say that Eve was literally created out of Adam's rib, that Noah had survived the flood in an ark in the year 2348 BC, and that the Tower of Babel was the cause of there being so many languages in the world.

The press made fun of Bryan when he said these things, and the judge refused to allow the questioning to continue. The jury then gave its verdict: Scopes was guilty of breaking the anti-evolution law. He was fined $100.

Work section

A. Test your understanding of this chapter by explaining the following terms: revivalists; theory of evolution; fundamentalists.

B. Can you think of any revivalist religious groups today which are similar to those you have read about in this chapter? How do they try to revive interest in the Christian religion?

C. Study the photograph above. Then, using the information you have read in this chapter, answer these questions:
1. The poster on the left of the photograph says 'Bryan's Books Here': who was Bryan?
2. What kinds of books do you think were on sale at this stall? Which book would you *not* expect to see on sale here?
3. Two of the posters are advertising a book called *Hell and the High Schools* by I.T. Martin. Judging by its title, what sort of message do you think I.T. Martin was trying to put across in his book?

D. Before going any further, make notes on what you have read in the last four chapters. Use points C, D, E and F of the revision guide on the next page if you are not sure how to organise your notes.

Revision guide

These note headings and sub-headings are not a complete set of notes to be copied. They should be used as a framework for notes which you make for yourself.

A. The American system of government
1. The Constitution
2. The system of federal government
3. The state governments
4. The Bill of Rights

B. The Presidents of the 1920s
1. Woodrow Wilson, 1913–21
2. Warren Harding, 1921–3
3. Calvin Coolidge, 1923–9
4. Herbert Hoover, 1929–33

C. Racial problems in the 1920s
1. The Immigration Laws
2. The Ku Klux Klan
3. The 'Back to Africa' movement

D. Political intolerance in the 1920s
1. Fear of communism
2. The Palmer raids of 1920
3. The Sacco and Vanzetti case

E. Prohibition and violence
1. The Anti-Saloon League
2. The Eighteenth Amendment and the Volstead Act
3. The failure of prohibition
4. Gangs and violence

F. Religion in the 1920s
2. The revivalists
2. The fundamentalists
3. The 'Monkey Trial' of 1925

Revision exercises

Study this summary of the Bill of Rights, contained in the first ten amendments to the Constitution. Then answer the questions beneath.

Amendment 1   People have freedom of religious belief, freedom of speech, freedom of the press, freedom of assembly.

Amendment 2   People have the right to keep and to carry weapons.

Amendment 3   Soldiers cannot be quartered in people's homes in peacetime.

Amendment 4   People may not have their homes and property searched or seized without good reason.

Amendment 5   People may not be executed, imprisoned or fined except by due process of law.

Amendment 6   People accused of crimes must be given a public trial without delay. The jury must be impartial.

Amendment 7   Legal cases involving sums of more than $20 must be tried by a jury.

Amendment 8   Judges must not impose excessive fines or excessive bail, nor must they give cruel or unusual punishments.

Amendment 9   The above rights are not the only rights that people have.

Amendment 10   Any power not given to the federal government is held by the state governments.

A. Judging by what you have read in Part One of this book, do you think that any of the above rights were ignored on any of the following occasions?

    Amendment 1 in the trial of Johnny Scopes.
    Amendment 4 in the Palmer raids.
    Amendment 6 in the Sacco and Vanzetti Case.

Explain your answer fully in each case.

B. In your opinion, is drinking alcohol an 'inalienable right' (a right that cannot be taken away)? Do you think that the Prohibition of alcohol in 1920 infringed Amendment 9 of the Constitution? Explain your answers.

C. From what you have read so far in this book, do you think that America in the 1920s deserved its reputation as a 'sweet land of liberty'? Explain your answer.

PART TWO

THE PURSUIT OF HAPPINESS?

A construction worker on the Metropolitan Life Building. Skyscrapers like this were a symbol of America's prosperity in the 1920s

One of the rights of Americans mentioned in the Declaration of Independence is liberty. You have by now decided how much liberty Americans enjoyed in the 1920s. Another right mentioned in the Declaration is the 'pursuit of happiness'. Part Two of this book invites you to decide how far Americans were able to achieve happiness in the 1920s.

For many people, the 1920s were exciting years,

often called the Roaring Twenties. It was the 'Jazz Age' when the music and film industries boomed, when skylines were changed by giant skyscrapers, and when cheap cars, radios and electrical goods changed the way in which people lived. After the suffering of the Great War, it seemed to many Americans that they could enjoy themselves as never before.

7

THE JAZZ AGE

Police in Chicago arrest bathers for being indecently dressed, July 1922

The two young women in the photograph above are **flappers**. Flappers, the fashionable young women of the 1920s, shocked older people by nearly everything they did. These young women in the photograph have shocked the onlookers by bathing 'semi-nude' in one-piece swimsuits on a Chicago beach.

Flappers shocked their parents and other older people in all sorts of ways. They wore short, bobbed hair and, worse, had it cut in men's barbers' shops instead of by ladies' hair dressers. They wore short skirts, backless gowns, and silk stockings rolled just above the knee. The President of Florida University had this to say about them:

'The low-cut gowns, the rolled hose [*stockings*] and short skirts are born of the devil and all his angels and are carrying the present and future generations to destruction.'

There were other objections to flappers. They smoked cigarettes in public. They went out with men without chaperones. They danced, holding their partners, without gloves. They went for all-night drives in motor cars, and some of them had sex before they were married. Worried American mothers formed an 'Anti-Flirt League' to protest against the behaviour of the flappers.

16

But the flappers were a sign of the times and the Anti-Flirt League failed to correct their behaviour. After the hardship and the horrors of the Great War young Americans wanted to enjoy themselves. New, exciting forms of music and dance became popular. **Jazz** music was the most popular music of the 1920s, which is why the 1920s are often called 'the Jazz Age'. Jazzmen such as Louis Armstrong, Benny Goodman and Fats Waller made big money out of night club performances and from records of their music.

To go with the new music came new dances. The Charleston, invented in the Jungles Casino in Charleston, South Carolina, was the favourite dance of the twenties. The One Step, the Black Bottom and the Tango were also popular. The new dances shocked many people, as you can see from this article in *The Catholic Telegraph*:

'The music is sensuous, the embracing of partners – the female only half-dressed – is absolutely indecent, and the motions – they are such as may not be described, with any respect for propriety, in a family newspaper. Suffice it to say that there are certain houses appropriate for such dances, but these houses have been closed by law.'

In the search for fun in the Jazz Age, millions of people went in for '**crazes**'. First there was a craze for mah-jong, a Chinese board game, then crossword puzzles became all the rage. When that died out, the craze was for marathon dancing and flagpole sitting: people entered competitions to see how long they could dance without stopping, or how long they could sit on top of a flagpole. 'Shipwreck Kelly' was the champion, setting a record of twenty-three days sitting on a flagpole.

Finally, the twenties were a golden age for American **sport**. Many of America's best-ever athletes won fame and fortune in the twenties, and set almost unbreakable records. Babe Ruth in baseball hit more home runs than anyone before him, while Bobby Jones, the greatest amateur golfer of the time, won both the British and American amateur and open contests in the same year.

Louis Armstrong's 'Hot Five', one of the best known jazz bands of the 1920s, photographed in 1926. Armstrong, centre, later married the pianist, Lil Hardin

Work section

A. Test your understanding of this chapter by explaining the following terms: flappers; the Anti-Flirt League; jazz; the Charleston; crazes.

B. Study the extract above from *The Catholic Telegraph*, then answer these questions:
1. For what reasons did the writer dislike jazz music and dances?
2. How would you try to defend jazz music and dancing against this sort of criticism?
3. Look at the photograph above of Louis Armstrong's 'Hot Five'. Can you think of another reason why many Americans disapproved of jazz music?

C. Study the photograph opposite of two flappers being arrested. What aspects of the flappers' appearance and behaviour do you think the onlookers found shocking?

17

'COOLIDGE PROSPERITY': THE BOOM OF THE AMERICAN ECONOMY

A seaside resort close to Boston, Massachusetts, 4 July 1926. Most of the cars are Model T Fords

Calvin Coolidge, President of America from 1923 to 1929, said 'the business of America is business'. During his presidency business boomed, and America became the richest country in the world. What caused this period of 'Coolidge prosperity' and how did it affect people's lives?

The motor car industry

The greatest business boom took place in the motor

car industry. There were three big car producers in the 1920s – Ford, Chrysler and General Motors. By far the biggest was the Henry Ford Motor Company.

Henry Ford, son of an Irish immigrant, and his Dutch wife, started making a **Model T** car in 1909. It was slow, ugly and difficult to drive, but for the next eighteen years this car, the 'Tin Lizzie', was America's best selling car.

The big attraction of the Model T Ford was its price: not only did the price never increase, it also kept dropping. Costing $1200 in 1909, the price in 1928 was only $295. As a result, fifteen million people were able to buy Model Ts between 1909 and 1928. By 1928 there was one car to every 4.5 people in America. To put it another way, one family in three owned at least one car.

Henry Ford was able to sell cars cheaply because they were mass-produced and standardised. By producing large numbers of cars on an assembly line Ford needed fewer workers, and that cut the cost of paying wages. By standardising the product (only one colour and one engine size were available) he cut production costs even further.

The car industry, more than any other, helped to make America prosperous in the 1920s. Car-making used up 20 per cent of America's steel, 80 per cent of her rubber, 75 per cent of her plate glass, and 65 per cent of her leather. The more cars were made, the more jobs there were in these industries. Cars on the road used seven billion gallons of petrol a year, and this made the oil producers of Texas rich. New roads had to be built for the increased traffic and this meant jobs for the construction industry. And along the new roads sprang up thousands of garages, 'gas stations', restaurants, 'motels', hot-dog stands – all providing even more jobs.

There were, however, problems that came with the motor car, as a retired businessman, Thomas Adams, remembered half a century later:

A. 'I think the country was in greater danger during the twenties than at any other time in my life. It seemed as though America had realised the American dream: more money every year for everybody. Within a few years, roughly from 1918 to 1924, everything utterly changed. Suddenly everybody owned a motor car. It seemed as though we were all liberated by Henry Ford. All we needed was to make more automobiles and build bigger houses. Then we began to realise that along with all Ford cars came dust, dirt, automobile crashes and the inevitable problems of the assembly line.'

Critics of the motor car said that the assembly line made workers into unskilled slaves, doing boring and unrewarding work. Some critics also pointed to the fact that gangsters were able to use 'getaway cars' to escape justice. They also called the car 'a house of prostitution on wheels' when it became common for lovers to do their courting on car back seats.

Consumer goods

During the 1920s the average pay of industrial workers doubled. Much of the extra income was spent on consumer goods. This also helped business to boom.

There were many new 'gadgets' which people wanted to buy, goods which we take for granted today but which were unusual then. In 1920 America's first radio station, Station KDKA, went on the air. Within a year radio became a craze, and by 1929 ten million homes had radio sets. Over 900,000 people bought refrigerators. Sales of vacuum cleaners, irons, ovens and telephones rocketed. The more people bought consumer goods like these, the more jobs there were in the industries that made them.

Hopes for the future

By the end of the twenties, most Americans took their prosperity for granted. They thought business would boom for ever. Herbert Hoover said in a speech in 1928:

B. 'One of the oldest and perhaps the noblest of human aspirations [hopes] has been the abolition of poverty . . . We in America today are nearer to the final triumph over poverty than ever before in the history of any land.'

Unfortunately America was nowhere near a 'final triumph over poverty'. As we shall see, there was terrible poverty in the midst of the plenty that Hoover spoke about. Worse, that poverty was to spread to every part of America within the next two years.

Work section

A. Study the photograph on the opposite page, then answer the following questions:
   1. List the advantages of car ownership that you can see in the photograph. Then make a list of the disadvantages you can see.
   2. Why were so many Americans able to become car-owners in the 1920s?

B. Study the comments made in source A.
   1. What, according to this businessman, was 'the American dream'?
   2. What do you think he meant by 'It seemed as though we were all liberated by Henry Ford'? (Look at the photograph opposite for ideas about how cars can 'liberate' people.)
   3. What, in this man's opinion, were the problems created by cars? In your opinion, do these problems outweigh the advantages of cars? Explain your answer.

C. Study the extract from a speech by Herbert Hoover (source B). Judging by what you have read in this chapter, why do you think Hoover believed that America in 1928 was close to 'the final triumph over poverty'?

9

HEROES AND MOVIE STARS

There are many heroes in American history. Most of them are men who helped to shape the country in its infancy. Early hunters like Daniel Boone and Kit Carson live on in American legend because they seem to represent all that is best about Americans – toughness, independence, bravery, self-reliance.

Americans in the 1920s had a passion for heroes. Perhaps the most famous of them was a young aircraft pilot, Charles A. Lindbergh.

'The Flying Fool'

In 1919 a New York businessman offered a prize of $25,000 to whoever flew non-stop from New York to Paris for the first time. On 20 May 1927 Captain Charles A. Lindbergh set out to win the prize. He took off from New York in a small, one-engined plane called *Spirit of St Louis*. He took no map and no parachute. With him in the open cockpit he had five sandwiches, two pints of water and an inflatable raft. Some reporters covering the story called him 'the flying fool'.

Charles A. Lindbergh and his plane, Spirit of St Louis, *in 1927*

Thirty-three and a half hours later Lindbergh touched down safely at Le Bourget, near Paris. Americans went almost mad with joy. When Lindbergh returned to America a week later, half a million letters and 75,000 telegrams were waiting for him. During a victory parade through New York, office workers gave him a 'ticker-tape welcome' by throwing confetti made of torn-up paper from their office windows (see the photograph on the cover of this book). 1800 tons of paper fell on to the streets along the route.

Lindbergh soon became America's greatest hero of the twentieth century. Hundreds of streets were renamed after him. He could not send his clothes to the cleaners because laundry workers kept them as souvenirs. He could not write cheques because people kept them for his autograph instead of cashing them. And the whole country mourned five years later when his baby son was kidnapped and brutally murdered.

Why was Lindbergh so popular? An English historian, Daniel Snowman, has explained his popularity in these terms:

> 'His achievement was one of the very few that managed to wed the dazzling scientific advances of a . . . progressive age to the . . . values of the past. On the one hand, he had obviously done something that required . . . great technological skill. On the other hand, Lindbergh himself epitomised [*stood for*] – in his healthy and rugged appearance, his self-effacing charm, his physical courage – all the legendary American virtues.'

Movie stars

In 1930 100 million Americans a week were 'going to the movies' to watch films. In Hollywood, a suburb of Los Angeles, film studios churned out hundreds of films each year to feed the appetites of movie-goers. The most important part of this film making business was what studio bosses called the **star system**.

Until 1910 performers in films were never named. Leading actresses were called such things as the 'Vitagraph Girl' and the 'Biograph Girl' after the film companies they worked for. Then Carl Laemmle, a film producer, decided to advertise a film by naming the 'Biograph Girl' who was in it. She was Florence Lawrence, and the next time she appeared in public her admirers mobbed her and tore her clothes. Box office takings for the films in which she appeared soared.

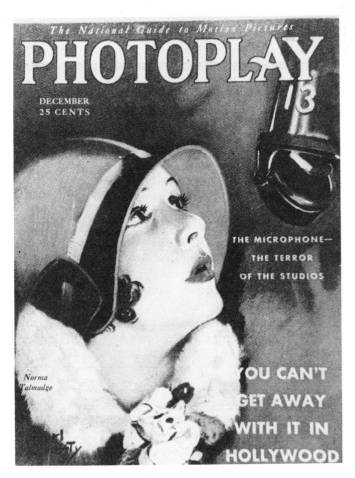

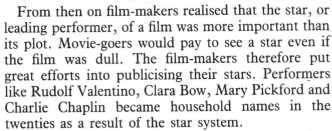

A fan magazine of 1929

Rudolf Valentino starring in The Sheik

From then on film-makers realised that the star, or leading performer, of a film was more important than its plot. Movie-goers would pay to see a star even if the film was dull. The film-makers therefore put great efforts into publicising their stars. Performers like Rudolf Valentino, Clara Bow, Mary Pickford and Charlie Chaplin became household names in the twenties as a result of the star system.

Fans worshipped their stars. When Rudolf Valentino died in 1926, aged 31, huge crowds queued for over a mile to see his embalmed body. Hysterical fans collapsed in grief and dozens were injured when a riot broke out among the mourners.

Until 1927 films were silent. Then *The Jazz Singer*, the first-ever 'talking film', came out. Soon all films were 'talkies' and many silent screen stars lost their jobs because they had strange accents or funny voices.

Why were the stars so popular? Partly it was because they provided millions of people with cheap entertainment. But movies also educated people. Ernst Lubitsch, a Hollywood film director, observed that American audiences were most interested in learning what cutlery to use, what hair styles to wear and how to mix cocktails. The stars were popular because they showed people how to behave.

Work section

A. Read the account by Daniel Snowman of why Charles Lindbergh was so popular:
 1. Give examples, taken from Chapter 8, of 'dazzling scientific advances' made in the 1920s.
 2. In what ways do you think Lindbergh's flight required 'great technological skill'?
 3. What 'legendary American virtues' do you think Americans saw in Charles Lindbergh?

B. Give two reasons why film stars were so popular in the 1920s.

C. Look at the magazine cover above.
 1. What do you think is the meaning of the caption 'The microphone – the terror of the studios'?
 2. Why do you think the microphone has the number thirteen written on it?
 3. What do you think it was that 'You can't get away with' in Hollywood? Explain your answer.

10
'ANYONE CAN BE RICH . . .'

'Suppose a man . . . begins a regular savings of $15 a month . . . If he invests in common stocks [*company shares*] . . . he will, at the end of twenty years, have at least $80,000 and an income from investments of around $400. I am firm in my belief that anyone can not only be rich, but ought to be rich.' (John J. Raskob, Director of General Motors, 1928)

John J. Raskob was one of America's best known businessmen, and several million Americans did exactly what he suggested. They invested their money in stocks and shares and in property.

The Florida land boom, 1924–6

Florida, the 'Sunshine State' in the south-east of the USA (see map on page 2), was a poor state at the start of the 1920s. Much of it was swamp land, with alligators, mosquitos and snakes. Yet between 1924 and 1926 some two million people went to Florida, hoping to buy land there.

The Florida land boom started in 1924 when estate agents advertised land for sale in new developments on the coast. This advertisement was typical:

'Go to Florida . . . where you sit and watch at twilight the graceful palm, latticed against the fading gold of the sun-kissed sky . . . where the whispering breeze springs fresh from the lap of the Caribbean.'

People began to buy land in Florida thinking it would be a holiday paradise, especially in winter when it was 20°C warmer than New York. At first the price of land was low, so even people without much money could afford to buy it. A 10 per cent deposit, called a '**binder**', gave them the right to buy the land when they had enough money.

So many people wanted to buy land that prices rose fast. People who had bought binders cheaply made big profits by selling them to new buyers. The new buyers in their turn could resell the binders for a big profit.

In 1925 binders were changing hands for a hundred times their original value. And new buyers were still coming to Florida, hoping to make fortunes. But the advertisements that attracted them were often false. Land advertised as being 'on the shore' was often 20 kilometres inland. A company called Manhattan Estates advertised land 'not more than three fourths of a mile from the prosperous and fast growing town of Nettie' – but Nettie was in fact a disused group of workmen's huts in a forest.

Gradually buyers realised they were being cheated. Suddenly nobody wanted to buy land, so its price dropped. Then a hurricane swept through Florida killing 400 people and wrecking everything in its path. Land prices fell to their original levels and buyers who had spent their life savings on dream homes were ruined.

The sea front in Miami, 1926, at the height of the Florida land boom

The front page of The New York Times of 15 July 1928

Copyright, 1928, by The New York Times Company   SUNDAY, JULY 15, 1928.

NATION-WIDE FEVER OF STOCK SPECULATION

Eager Buying Has Reached All Classes of People Throughout the Country and Has Set New Records In Many Directions—Effects of Struggle to Grasp Profits in Trading in Securities Are Evident

By CHARLES McD. PUCKETTE.

Playing the stock market

Study this table of the prices of shares in ten American companies:

	3 March 1928	3 Sept. 1929
American Can	¢ 77	¢182
Anaconda Copper	¢ 54	¢162
Electric Bond and Share	¢ 90	¢204
General Electric	¢129	¢396
General Motors	¢140	¢182
New York Central	¢160	¢256
Radio	¢ 94	¢505
United States Steel	¢138	¢279
Westinghouse E & M	¢ 92	¢313
Woolworth	¢181	¢251

You can easily see that between March 1928 and September 1929 the prices of shares rose a great deal. A person who bought any of these shares in 1928 was able to make a big profit by selling them in 1929.

Usually it is businessmen who invest in shares. They buy them in large numbers at a stock exchange, hoping to share in any profits that the company makes. They buy a company's shares when they think it is likely to make a profit, and they sell the shares if the company is doing badly.

In America in 1928 share-buying was quite different. Ordinary people without much cash were investing their savings on the stock exchange. They were able to do this because **stockbrokers**, the dealers in shares, would accept a 10 per cent deposit, called a **margin**, on the cost of the shares. So if a nurse, for example, with $100 in savings wanted to invest in shares, she could buy $1000 worth of shares 'on the margin'.

Why were brokers prepared to sell shares on the margin? They were confident that share prices would go on rising, so the people to whom they lent money would make enough profit to repay them with interest.

By 1929 more than a million Americans owned shares. Playing the stock market was almost a national hobby, like betting on horses or doing football pools. But unlike the pools, everybody won on the stock exchange – for a while. For a while, anyone really could be rich.

Work section

A. Test your understanding of this chapter by explaining the following terms: binder; stocks; margin; stockbroker.

B. Study the table of share prices above, and imagine that you have bought 100 shares in the Woolworth Company.
   1. How much would 100 Woolworth shares cost you in 1928? (Multiply the share price by 100.)
   2. How much profit would you make if you sold your shares on 3 September 1929? (Multiply the 1929 price by 100, then subtract the amount you paid for them in 1928.)
   3. Which of the shares in the table above made the most profit between 1928 and 1929? Which of these shares would you have bought?
   4. How could you, as an ordinary person without large savings, have bought shares in these companies in 1928?

C. Study the advertisement on the opposite page for land in Florida.
   1. How convincing do you find it?
   2. Do you think many Americans were attracted to Florida by this advertisement? If not, what do you think did attract them?

D. Make revision notes on what you have read in Part Two of this workbook. There is a revision guide on the next page to help you.

Revision guide

These note headings and sub-headings are not a complete set of notes to be copied. They should be used as a framework for notes which you make for yourself. They follow straight on from the notes you have already made.

G. The Jazz Age
1. Flappers
2. Music and dancing
3. Crazes
4. Sport

H. The boom of the American economy
1. Motor car production
2. Consumer goods
3. Hopes for the future

I. Heroes and movie stars
1. Charles Lindbergh
2. The star system

J. Speculation and investment
1. The Florida land boom
2. Playing the stock market

Revision exercise

Historians have used many 'labels' to describe America in the 1920s: the Jazz Age, the New Era, the Roaring Twenties, the Age of Excess, the New Freedom, the Age of Wonderful Nonsense.

Make a table like the one below, putting each of these labels into the left hand column. Using the information you have read so far in this book, fill the right hand column with examples of why each label can be used to describe the twenties.

When you have finished, decide for yourself which label best describes America in the twenties.

Example:

The New Era	There were many *new* developments in the twenties. Car ownership became common. *New* kinds of consumer goods like radios, vacuum cleaners, refrigerators etc. changed many people's lives. There were many *new* forms of entertainment, such as talking films, jazz music, dancing the Charleston, and listening to the radio.

PART THREE

THE GREAT DEPRESSION

A German cartoon called 'World Economic Conference, 1927'. Rich bankers and businessmen ignore the poor while they themselves are on the brink of ruin

You have found out that America in the Roaring Twenties was the richest country in the world. Life for many Americans was more comfortable than ever before. It seemed as if there was nothing to stop everyone from being rich.

But a few people were not so sure. Some bankers and economists warned the government that the good times would not last for ever. The cartoonist who drew the cartoon above obviously shared their point of view.

In 1929 the good times did come to an end and an economic depression began. During the 'Great Depression' millions of Americans lost their jobs, their homes and their possessions. Within three years the Americans ceased to be the richest people on earth and became some of the poorest.

11

THE CAUSES OF THE GREAT DEPRESSION

Historians do not know exactly what caused the Great Depression. Like all important events in history, it had many causes. However, most historians would agree that four major problems in the American economy helped to bring it about.

Poverty in the midst of plenty

Study this table showing what four groups of American workers earned in 1929:

Average monthly earnings of workers in 1929		
Farmers in South Carolina	$129	(£29)
Town workers in South Carolina	$412	(£92)
Town workers in New York	$881	(£196)
Fruit farmers in California	$1246	(£227)

It is obvious from these figures that not everyone grew rich in the 'Roaring Twenties'. A cotton farmer in South Carolina earned almost ten times less than a fruit farmer in California.

Another survey of what people earned in 1929 showed that

- 60 per cent of American families earned less than $2000 (£440) a year, the minimum needed for the basic necessities of life.
- One third of personal income was earned by the top 5 per cent of wealthy Americans.

In other words, the wealth of America was spread very unequally among its citizens. The majority lived in poverty while a small minority were very rich.

This helped cause the Great Depression because only the well-off could afford to buy the goods made in American factories. Once they had all bought cars, radios, vacuum cleaners and other consumer goods, the demand for these things dropped, so the factories had to make fewer of them. This meant laying off workers, causing unemployment to rise.

The problems of farmers

A second cause of the Great Depression lay on America's farms. New farm machinery such as tractors and combine harvesters helped American farmers to produce more food in the twenties than they had ever produced before. However, they produced more food than the population could eat, so they were left with **surplus** food. This caused food prices to drop and that meant lower incomes for farmers and farm workers.

Farmers tried to keep up their incomes by growing even more food, but this made food prices fall even lower: the bigger the surplus, the lower the price.

Thousands of farmers tried to get out of their difficulties by borrowing money from banks. Farmers took out mortgages worth $2000 million during the twenties. But this simply made their problems worse. As their incomes continued to drop they could not repay their mortgages. When that happened the banks ended their mortgages and threw them off their land.

By 1929 millions of farmers and farm workers were out of work and hungry. It was no help to them that there was more food in America than people could eat. In areas where they grew only oranges, for example, they could not live on oranges alone, so they starved.

Trade problems

Why could America not solve these problems by selling her surplus food and goods to other countries?

The reason was that in 1923 the government had put **tariffs**, or customs duties, on foreign goods coming into America. The government did this to help American industry: tariffs made foreign goods more expensive than American goods, so people naturally bought American goods in the shops.

The disadvantage of this was that the governments of other countries did exactly the same. They put tariffs on foreign goods coming into their countries, so American businessmen found it hard to sell their goods abroad. This did not matter as long as Americans could consume everything made in America. But it did matter in 1929 when there were huge surpluses of goods that they could not consume. The surpluses could not be sold abroad.

Speculation on the stock market

As you know, from reading Chapter 10, around a million Americans were investing in company shares in the late 1920s. Many were ordinary people, buying shares 'on the margin'. It was easy to buy some shares, wait for the price to rise and then sell them for a profit. It was a guaranteed way of making lots of money – as long as share prices kept rising and as long as there were people who wanted to buy shares.

Unfortunately, this kind of speculation, or investment in shares, was another cause of the Great Depression. The problem was that too many people were buying shares with borrowed money. Investor X, for example, would buy $1000 worth of shares on

Buyers in a stockbroker's office watch clerks chalking up even higher prices for shares

the margin. He would then sell them for $1500 to Investor Y who paid him with a credit note, or IOU. Y would then sell the shares for $2000 to Investor Z who paid him with money borrowed on the margin. Y could then repay X his $1500 and keep $500 as profit for himself.

This system of **credit** worked well as long as everybody was confident that share prices would go on rising. But supposing investors began to doubt that shares were worth the price being asked? They would want to sell, not buy shares. And they would want to sell them for cash, not for credit notes.

Doubts about share prices began to spread in 1928. Many companies were unable to sell the goods they were making, so their profits went down. That meant that investors were less keen to buy their shares. Some rich investors quietly began to sell large numbers of their shares, thinking that some share values were too high.

Suddenly, in October 1929, everybody was trying to sell their shares. Panic spread on the Wall Street Stock Exchange in New York as share prices began to fall steeply. As we shall see, this panic brought about the **Wall Street Crash**.

Work section

A. Test your understanding of this chapter by explaining the following terms: surplus; tariff; credit; depression.

B. Study this American cartoon of Christmas 1928, then answer the questions beneath.

'D'ya think you'll be workin' by next year, Papa?'

1. Judging by what you have read in this chapter, what kind of job might a man like the one in the cartoon have had before becoming unemployed? Explain your answer.
2. For what reasons were many Americans out of work by 1928?
3. Why would the answer to the boy's question most likely be 'no'? Explain your answer.
4. What message, in your opinion, was the cartoonist trying to put across?

12
THE WALL STREET CRASH

Wall Street is on Manhattan Island in the heart of New York City. As you can see from the photograph below, it is a street of tall office buildings. The most important of these buildings is the New York **Stock Exchange** where stocks and shares of all kinds are bought and sold.

'Black Thursday'

On a good day in the Wall Street Stock Exchange some two or three million stocks and shares might be bought and sold, while a company's shares might go up a few points, or cents, in value. On a bad day a company's shares might go down two or three points.

On Thursday 24 October 1929 share prices on Wall Street fell faster and lower than at any other time before or since. For this reason it is known as '**Black Thursday**'. As soon as the Stock Exchange opened its doors at nine in the morning, stockbrokers started selling shares in large numbers. By midday shares in even the strongest companies had gone down dozens of points. General Electric shares which had opened at 315 points fell to 283. United States Steel crashed from 205 to 193. Shares in Radio plummeted by 24 points.

Six of the richest bankers in New York hurriedly met to discuss this crisis. They agreed to spend $40 million each buying shares, hoping that this would encourage other people to buy shares rather than sell them. After all, if they were willing to spend $40 million each on shares, why shouldn't ordinary investors want to buy them too?

For a while the bankers' plan worked. When the Stock Exchange closed that afternoon, share prices had stopped falling. It seemed that the crisis was over.

But during the next few days, all sorts of strange rumours began to spread. It was said that eleven big shareholders who had lost fortunes that day had committed suicide by leaping from their skyscraper offices. There was also a rumour that the army was having to guard the Stock Exchange against an angry mob of ruined shareholders.

Wall Street after the crash. Anxious crowds have gathered outside the Stock Exchange, 29 October 1929, trying to find out what has happened to the value of their shares

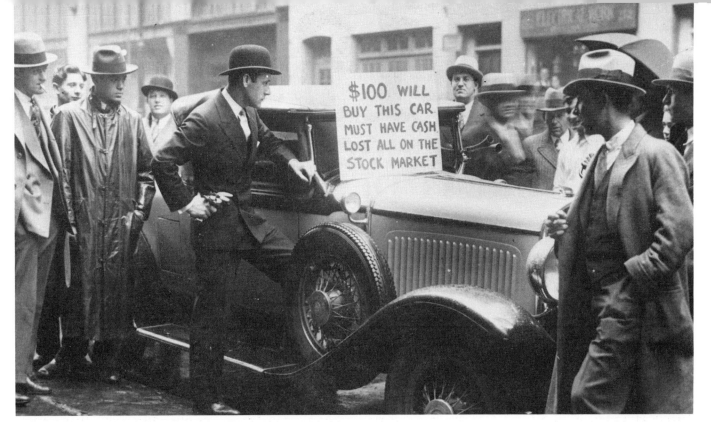

New York, October 1929. A ruined shareholder tries to raise some cash quickly

The final crash

Over the following weekend something happened which made another big fall in share prices certain. Many brokers who had sold shares 'on the margin' (see Chapter 10) had borrowed money from banks to buy the shares in the first place. The banks were now demanding repayment of their money. To repay the banks, the brokers in their turn had to ask their customers for more margin. And the only way in which their customers could pay more margin was to sell more shares.

So on Tuesday, 29 October, there was a mad scramble to sell shares – at any price. Panic-stricken brokers and investors sold over 16 million shares during the day. The average price of shares fell 40 points and shareholders lost a total of $8000 million.

The Stock Market did not recover from this. Share prices kept on dropping until they reached rock bottom in November 1929, as this table shows:

	3 Sept. 1929	13 Nov. 1929
American Can	¢182	¢ 86
Anaconda Copper	¢162	¢ 70
Electric Bond and Share	¢204	¢ 50
General Electric	¢396	¢168
General Motors	¢182	¢ 36
New York Central	¢256	¢160
Radio	¢505	¢ 28
United States Steel	¢279	¢150
Westinghouse E & M	¢313	¢102
Woolworth	¢251	¢ 52

Work section

A. Test your understanding of this chapter by explaining the following terms: Wall Street; Stock Exchange; Black Thursday.

B. Study the photograph above, then answer these questions.
1. What evidence is there in the photograph that the seller of the car made a lot of money on the stock market before the Wall Street crash?
2. The seller of the car wrote 'must have cash' on his poster; what might he need cash for at this time?
3. How likely do you think the seller of the car was to find a buyer? Explain your answer.

C. Study the list of share prices above, then answer these questions:
1. Look back to question B3 on page 23. Which company's shares did you decide to buy?
2. What has happened to the price of the shares you bought as a result of the Wall Street crash?
3. Supposing that you did not sell your shares before the crash, how much money have you lost on these shares?

PRESIDENT HOOVER AND THE GREAT DEPRESSION

New York, December 1931. A 'breadline' of unemployed men waiting for free food from the Municipal Lodging House

The Wall Street Crash of 1929 made the Great Depression in America much worse. Many banks which had put their customers' money into shares now went bankrupt. Thousands of companies whose shares were now worthless went out of business, putting even more people out of work.

The effects of the Depression

By the winter of 1932 America was in deep economic trouble, as these figures show. In 1932

- Twelve million people were out of work – a quarter of the country's entire work force.
- The number of people out of work was going up at the rate of 12,000 *every day*.
- 20,000 companies went bankrupt.
- 1616 banks closed down.
- One farmer in every twenty was thrown off his land for failure to make mortgage repayments.
- 23,000 people committed suicide, the largest yearly figure in American history.

An American journalist who travelled around America in 1932 said this about the condition of the country:

A. 'In the State of Washington I was told that the forest fires raging in the region all summer and fall [autumn] were caused by unemployed timber workers and bankrupt farmers in an endeavor to earn a few honest dollars as fire fighters. The last thing I saw on the night I left Seattle was numbers of women searching for scraps of food in the refuse piles . . .
While Oregon sheep farmers fed mutton to buzzards I saw men picking for meat scraps in the garbage cans in the cities of New York and Chicago . . . We have overproduction and underconsumption at the same time and in the same country.'

Of all the problems facing Americans in the Depression, **unemployment** was much the worst. There was no system of government benefits for the unemployed. Hungry, out-of-work people had to turn to charities such as the 'Holy Name Mission' and the Salvation Army for help. In every city, long **breadlines** of silent, hopeless men and women queued for free handouts of bread and soup. In the countryside people ate wild berries and roots. Some actually starved to death.

Hoover and the Federal Government

As you know from Chapter 2 President Hoover believed in 'rugged individualism'. The government, he thought, should let people live their own lives, and leave them to sort out their own problems.

During the Great Depression Hoover therefore did little to help the unemployed. He said in 1932:

B. 'It is not the function of the government to relieve individuals of their responsibilities to their neighbors, or to relieve private institutions of their responsibilities to the public.'

Anyway, Hoover did not think the Depression would last long. 'Prosperity is just around the corner', he told a group of businessmen in 1932. In speeches he repeated his belief that there was nothing basically wrong with the economy.

Many people who had voted for Hoover in 1928 now said 'In Hoover we trusted, now we are busted'. They used his name in ways that showed they blamed him for the Depression. 'Hoovervilles' was the name they gave to shanty towns made of rubbish where homeless, out-of-work people lived. 'Hoover Stew' was the soup given out by the charity kitchens.

Hoover did take some steps to improve the American economy. In 1930 he cut taxes by $130 million. In 1931 he put money into building river dams such as the Hoover Dam. This created jobs in the construction industry and, in the long run, increased the electricity supply. In 1932 he signed the Emergency Relief and Reconstruction Act, giving $300 million to the states for helping the unemployed.

But even these few measures had little effect. Many Republicans in the states believed even more strongly than Hoover in 'rugged individualism'. They disliked the Federal Government in Washington poking its nose into their affairs, and they gave out only $30 million of the money offered to them.

In November 1932, in the Presidential election, the American voters voted Hoover out of office. In his place they elected a Democrat, Franklin D. Roosevelt, who bravely promised 'a New Deal for the American people'. Thirteen years of Republican rule in which America had risen to new heights of prosperity, and then crashed to the depths of depression, had come to an end.

Work section

A. Test your understanding of this chapter by explaining the following terms: breadlines; Hoovervilles; Emergency Relief and Reconstruction Act.

B. Study the evidence in source A.
1. Why, according to this journalist, were there many forest fires in the State of Washington in 1932?
2. Why do you think sheep farmers in Oregon fed mutton to buzzards instead of selling it?
3. What do you think the writer meant by 'We have overproduction and underconsumption at the same time in the same country'?

C. Read President Hoover's comment on unemployment (source B). Who, according to Hoover, was responsible for helping the unemployed? Why did he think it was not the government's job to help the unemployed?

D. Look at the photograph opposite. Bearing in mind that millions of women as well as men were unemployed in 1932, why do you think that only men are queuing up in this breadline?

E. Finish your work on America 1920–32 by making revision notes on the Great Depression. There is a revision guide on the next page to help you.

Revision guide

These note headings and sub-headings are a guide to organising your notes. They are not a complete set of notes to be copied. They follow straight on from the notes you have already made on America.

K. The causes of the Great Depression
  1. Poverty in the midst of plenty
  2. The problems of farmers
  3. Trade problems
  4. Speculation on the Stock Market

L. The Wall Street Crash
  1. Black Thursday, 24 October 1929
  2. The crash of share prices

M. Hoover and the Great Depression
  1. The effects of the Great Depression
  2. Hoover's policies in the Depression

Revision exercise

Study this cartoon. Using the information you have read in all three parts of this book, answer the questions beneath.

1. Uncle Sam is sitting in a chair marked 'luxury'. In what ways did Americans in the twenties live in 'luxury'?
2. Uncle Sam's grandchildren running around his chair each represent one bad aspect of America in the twenties. Give one example of each of these bad things: 'crime', 'graft' [*corruption*], 'scandal', 'materialism', 'indulgence'.
3. The smoke from Uncle Sam's cigar represents 'easy money'. In what ways could Americans make 'easy money' in the twenties?
4. In your own words, describe what you think is the point of this cartoon.

An American cartoon drawn for the Chicago Times *in September 1925. Uncle Sam, the symbol of America, looks back to the early days when pioneers lived simple lives in log cabins*